Poor Old Rabbit!

Cynthia Rider • Alex Brychta

OXFORD
UNIVERSITY PRESS

Floppy saw a toy rabbit.

"Poor old rabbit,"
said Floppy.

"Nobody wants it."

Floppy took it to Kipper.

"Poor old rabbit,"
said Kipper.

Kipper took it to Mum.

"Look at this rabbit,"
said Kipper.

"Nobody wants it."

"Poor old rabbit," said Mum.

Dad washed it.

Kipper brushed it.

Chip and Wilma mended it.

Everybody wanted it now.

Oh no!

"Poor old rabbit,"
said Kipper.

Why do you think somebody has put the rabbit in the bin?

Why isn't it always safe to take toys out of the bin in the park?

Why did everybody want the rabbit at the end of the story?

What is your favourite toy? What would you do if it got old and torn?

A maze

Help Kipper to get to the rabbit.

**Useful common words repeated in this story and
other books at Level 2.**

and   at   it   said   to   took   wants

Names: Mum   Dad   Biff   Chip   Kipper   Wilf   Wilma   Floppy